This book is not about feeling sorry for people. It's about the messes people create for others after they wander too far into the horrors of darkness, try to fight their way out by themselves, and completely lose direction. A few details have been changed for anonymity at this time.

If you suffer from depression or suicidal thoughts, get help from professionals who are trained in helping with these understandable afflictions. This book is no substitute for that and is not an attempt to fix anyone. The sole purpose is to persuade people to find help while they are still able to accept it, so they can also spare their loved ones terrible messes that last for years and years and years.

If Seth Murphy had read this account of the messes he would leave behind, he would not have followed through when he did. And perhaps he would have become convinced that it's a good idea to seek help. Instead, he lived behind a mask that worked all too well. This story of my cousin I will tell as a specialist in human learning and memory, and I hope you never forget it.

MAX T. RUSSELL

Before You Kill Yourself

A True Story about the UnDying Mess
Suicide Leaves Behind

Max T. Russell

DEDICATION

To two cousins, a nephew, an aunt, and a great-grandfather, all of whom left big messes that can never be cleaned up.

They didn't think of that.

CONTENTS

VISIT TO DEATH ROW

My grandpa once told me of a man who wanted to enter a coal mine where they both worked. Grandpa warned him not to open the door to the shaft, or the wind would trigger a fire inside. He said the wind was coming from a dangerous direction. The man opened the door. The wind rushed in. A plume of fire rushed out. The man fell down dead.

Seth Murphy had read such stories himself. He came from a long line of smart family. He knew how quickly mere humans are snuffed out when fire gobbles up oxygen or makes poisonous gases out of fabrics, walls, carpet, plastics – and gasoline. He would never feel a thing, at least not for more than a moment or two, which would be no big deal. Everybody has at least a few moments of discomfort in life. Shoot, some folks have severe pain for days, weeks, even months. Everything was calculated. Everything would end in a flash, and everyone would get over the sorrow of his loss soon enough. So had he calculated, and he was pretty good with numbers.

When Sandi Murphy visited Seth in prison, he was on death row. Sandi was horrified. Her son wouldn't harm a flea, and yet a strong chain connected the handcuffs on his wrists to the shackles on his ankles, allowing him just enough movement to walk where he was told to go. He moved cautiously. Sandi wanted to tear the blindfold right off his face. She didn't need anyone's permission. She was his mother!

She sat on a bench in the cell, watching through the solid door and wall. She could see right through them. The door opened and a female guard gently led Seth inside. He still didn't know his mother was there. He stood in front of her, facing the back wall, where Sandi sat. "I love you, Seth," she said. He stepped toward her and dropped to his knees on the concrete floor, buried his head in his mother's lap and cried and said he was sorry, he was so sorry, he was oh, so sorry.

But it was just another of Sandi's nightmares. Seth hadn't calculated the months of torture his mom would have to endure as she relived those awful visits to prison that never really happened but were as real as if they *had* happened, those awful, awful visits that gave shocking sensations of grief from watching her son so helpless, so isolated, so in pain, so alone in chains of captivity. Her nightmares dragged on for as long as many prisoners' sentences do, and whatever goes on inside the mind can be as real and vivid and terrifying as what, so to speak, never happened. Eight months would be, for instance, a long time to sit in your gasoline-soaked 1998 Mazda pickup and slowly sizzle.

Sometimes Sandi would wake up in the morning and not know what day it was.

For a long time I was confused all the way till lunch. It seemed like he was still alive, and I would have to remind myself that he was gone.

During those months of torment, Sandi couldn't function during the day, couldn't sleep at night. She quit caring about anything, simply because she couldn't care. It took everything in her just to keep a routine. Go to work, do her work, return home and retreat to the recliner that she had moved into her bedroom, away from all the other rooms where visitors or family might be, away from where anything might be. Her mother-in-law dedicated herself to making dinners and maintaining the Murphys' house, while Sandi fell apart in the recliner day after day, many times a day. She snacked at late hours and picked up twenty pounds. She had no motivation to get up and exercise; she was already doing the impossible – surviving one eternal hour at a time.

Seth's calculations had not allowed for this. The nature of his departure activated intolerably longlasting effects in his mother, not to mention in his sister, Maddie, and his father, Doug Murphy. Each family member manifested different effects, all rooted in grief, sustained depression, and hopelessness – the very problems Seth wanted to escape forever.

One thing Sandi stopped doing after Seth lit the match was to listen to music stations on the radio. For the first time ever, songs she had known for years sounded different. Almost every one of them reminded her of what she had lost, what could not be recovered, what could not be reversed, what could not be corrected, what could not be held in her arms. Words that had been simple vehicles for melody now throbbed simultaneously in her heart and brain with rhythmic rudeness, rhythmic coldness, rhythmic savagery, tearing at her, pulling at her, demanding confidential, dark interpretations.

I can't stop loving you. .... Time has stood still since we've been apart.

Drove my Chevy to the levy, but the levy was dry. ... This'll be the day that I die.

Where, oh where, can my baby be? The Lord has taken her away from me.

Richard Cory...went home and put a bullet through his head.

Billie Joe jumped off the Tallahatchie bridge.

But one thing there is missing in the picture. Without her face it seems so incomplete.

I'm leaving on a jet plane. I don't know when I'll be back again.

His dog up and died, he up and died. After twenty years he still grieved.

Yesterday all my troubles seemed so far away.

Every time I tried to tell you, the words just came out wrong.

Hey, it's good to be back home again.

Make me feel at home, while I miss my baby, while I miss my baby.

Keeps me searching for a heart of gold, and I'm gettin' old.

I feel so bad I've got a worried mind. I'm so lonesome all of the time.

He said, "Bill, I believe this is killing me."

There's a man with a gun over there, telling me I've got to beware.

Hands touching hands, reaching out… Good times never seemed so good.

I never knew lonely till you.

And when no hope was left inside on that starry, starry night…

Close your eyes and think of me, and soon I will be there.

Have I told you lately that I love you.

All the leaves are brown, and the sky is gray.

Even songs Sandi didn't really know were suddenly screaming at her.

Into this life we're born, and sometimes we don't know why.

Let me hold you one last time. ... Lord knows I feel like dying.

There's a garden, what a garden, only happy faces bloom there.

Now I know just how much I have lost. Yes, I lost my little darling...

Sometimes I have a great notion to jump into the river and drown.

Take your memory with you, so I won't have to miss you.

Johnny Cash's song spoke fresh messages of despair to Sandi and recalled Seth's final note.

Love is a burning thing. ... I fell into a burning ring of fire.

Well, I know I had it coming. I know I can't be free.

But the question is, To be true to who? 'Cause I ain't got no one to be true to.

Click.

There would be no more radio music for Seth's mother, another issue he had not calculated. From now on, Sandi would listen only to radio programs of conversation, newsy analysis, and other forms of talk. But the songs still chased her in the grocery store, the mall, on TV, in people's cars when she rode with them, on her daughter's radio, and in her own head. She had never noticed so many depressing statements that never meant a thing until now. How could dismal concepts, which lately crushed the heart, have been attached to so many good times of the past? How could they turn to poison? It didn't make sense! Sandi hardly paid attention to the words she sang back then. Now she couldn't ignore them.

CRIME SCENE

Seth's method for ending his existence caused his Mazda pickup and the area around it to be designated a crime scene. The little truck was engulfed in flames when the fire trucks arrived. Seth had opened the windows so the blaze could engorge itself on air, yet the confines of the interior kept the fire contained and completely lethal. That was enough to burn him beyond recognition, but his teeth, some yet unposted blogs, and a note still on his computer would eventually answer all questions. The crucial challenge for Sandi, Doug and Maddie, as well as for other relatives and friends, was that the legal process of establishing Seth's identity could not be rushed.

Nevertheless, the charred body that was discovered in the process of extinguishing the fire had to be him. Seth Murphy was six foot and over 200 pounds. He filled half the cab, and the truck was his. But his dental records needed to be compared against his teeth to verify he was the truck's occupant.

A day of that kind of waiting can seem like a thousand years, and a few moments can be eternity – another ravaging miscalculation. If Seth had succeeded in turning himself to ashes, things would have been worse. At least the police had his teeth.

The news media were already telling their versions of the story. Online newspaper readers were speculating in the Comments section. Even Seth's mother joined the conversation:

> He is a human being with a family who loves him dearly. A positive ID is required before the authorities can establish his identity, but I'm telling you as his mother that we already miss him. Please stop your guessing and speculating. We are going through unspeakable suffering.

The police department's official position was that information was still being collected and analyzed. Doug and Sandi were scrambling to get the dental records to prove identy and have their son's body released.

The Murphys went ahead and conducted a memorial service for Seth on January 19th, a week after his death – but not quite a week. The 19th was only six days after Friday the 13th, a date consistent with Seth's sense of humor. He was well liked for his good nature and humor. But the days since his passing were a long, burning hell for the Murphys who survived. They still didn't have official confirmation on dental records. They didn't even have the body. All they had were pictures of the friendly guy who torched himself on Friday the 13th beside a fire hydrant to make the firefighters' job a little easier. The irony was not humorous. It was not even good-natured. To the police, it pointed to premeditated self-destruction.

January 20 began a four-day holiday for many individuals and businesses, including the Murphy family's dentist, who left on vacation. Verifying Seth's identity would stop much of the ongoing speculation and commotion around the cause and the context of his final deed. The Murphys were able to reach a hygienist, who was able to enter the office and get the dental records. Investigators could now attribute the teeth to the food lover whose motto was "Give me my seafood."

THE SECOND CALL FROM THE DETECTIVE

The Murphys were beginning to settle into a "new normal" when February came. The memorial service had helped a great deal in their initial healing, now that there was no argument about whether Seth was gone. They were also in the third week of seeing a licensed counselor. A particularly vital source of comfort was knowing with certainty that Seth's death was actually an accident, not suicide, as the police continued to believe.

Doug's cell phone rang at 9 p.m. on Friday of the first week of the new normal. A police detective said he had found a suicide note on Seth's computer. Doug passed out on the bed, eyes wide open, mouth agape. Sandi thought he'd had a heart attack. She screamed to rouse him. Doug regained consciousness. But the detective's discovery, which confirmed what the police suspected, was a great setback for the family. It shattered them.

Newspapers had originally reported possible indications of homicide. Some people had speculated online that drugs might have been involved. For the Murphys, the publicity was indeed throwing fuel on the fire.

Then Seth's name was announced on the evening news only two days after the incident. The police had told the Murphys that official, positive identification would take four weeks, and they kept their word. But someone had leaked the name. A friend told Sandi she heard it on TV. Angry that the family's privacy had been circumvented, Sandi called the station. A woman answered.

"Hello, I want to talk to someone in management," Mrs. Murphy said.

"Can I help you?" the other woman asked.

Sandi explained her reason for calling.

"Oh, I worked on that story. I'll be happy to talk to you about it."

Sandi flew into a rage. "You worked on that story? That was irresponsible reporting! How can you call yourself a media professional? You have been inconsiderate of our privacy and you have put your quest for fast information above our feelings and the facts!"

The reporter was silent.

"Who was your source?" Mrs. Murphy continued. "Where did you get your information? I demand to know your source!"

The reporter panicked. "I got my information from the fire department."

"I'm going to talk to the fire department then!" said Mrs. Murphy.

"You're going to leave my name out of it, aren't you?"

"I'll leave your name out."

Sandi called the police department the next day and was told the fire department did not release her son's identity to the media. Several days later, Sandi came across an article in the newspaper describing how Seth had died. The report, based on the autopsy, said the cause of death was smoke inhalation; that is to say, everything that smoke may contain – poisonous gases included – and the removal of oxygen.

The Murphys had been waiting desperately for such information. They wanted assurance that Seth's pain in death had not been prolonged and severe – as their own would be.

The police were still trying to ascertain the cause of the fire. Suicide note or not, the investigation continued to follow every lead. Seth had recently taken the truck to a repair shop because of an ignition problem. Could that have caused the fire? If so, how in the world could that be? The truck's interior would not explode into a ball of fire without a great deal of help from a fuel source, and that would not be the gas tank.

Seth left a clue. Just before he left his apartment and settled one last time as comfortably as possible into the driver's seat of his pickup, he went into his Facebook account and posted a phrase from T.S. Eliot's poem, "The Hollow Men":

This is the way the world ends: not with a bang but a whimper.

Seth planned no violence to anyone in his leaving. He would not storm angrily out of the world, taking others down with him. He was a pacifist. His profile on an online community said so. His world would end with a whimper of the same tone carried by the empty, aimless, masked hollow men with hollow lives and hollow meaning whom Eliot had described in raw terms that struck a harmonizing chord with Seth. Seth had already written a great deal about this unrealistic perception of himself, but the Murphys didn't know yet, even though Seth had meant for everyone to know.

THE FIRST CALL FROM THE DETECTIVE

At 7 a.m. on Friday the 13th while television, newspaper and radio were on the scene to cover the departing whimper, Sandi was on her way to work, with Maddie along to be dropped off at the high school. The freshman was trying to get 20 minutes of sleep. The car radio announced that fire crews had put out an early-morning inferno inside a small Mazda pickup. A body was discovered in the driver's seat. It was burned beyond recognition. Identification would have to wait for an investigation.

Maddie opened her eyes and shifted in her seat. Sandi thought of Maddie's brother. *Well,* she told herself, *we parents are this way. We think about our kids every time we hear these scary news reports. Let's see now, Seth worked second shift last night, so he would've gone to bed and is still asleep.*

Mama reached into her purse for her cell phone and then pulled her hand back. *No, I'm not going to call to check on him and wake him up and make him mad at me for being a panicky mother. He's a big boy. He's 29. He just got a promotion at the home hardware company. If he were involved, the police would've told me.*

Maddie was sinking back into a slumber. Sandi was moving down the highway toward the high school. She relaxed and prepared for a day at the realty office. The 30-minute commute from the Murphy residence in Stickney, a village located southeast of the Chicago city limits, always helped her get an early focus on the day.

The police detectives were trying to reconcile information. The license plates on the pickup truck were in Doug's name. He had cosigned for the truck loan, and he and Seth lived in different counties. The detectives called Doug's boss at work. The boss then asked Doug if he owned a Mazda pickup. Doug answered no. "I didn't think you did," his boss said, "but a detective is on the phone and he wants to talk to you about the truck."

The detective told Doug about the fire and said he didn't know if it was an accident, foul play, or suicide.

The world turned mute inside Doug's head as his boss drove him to the realty office so he could give Sandi the news firsthand. The day he adopted Sandi's only son, of eight years, was one of the happiest days of his life. Seth always called him *Daddy*, and the love between the two was obvious to all. Doug said the reason was simple.

It was because he was my son. That's not just something you say. It's something you live each and every day. Being a father is about being there – and I *was* there.

The receptionist went to Sandi's office and motioned for her to come along. Sandi followed partway down the hall and stopped.

"What is it? Tell me what's wrong! What is it?"

The receptionist turned around. "I don't know, but Doug says he has to talk to you *now*."

Now. That was a code word between Doug and Sandi, their private way of communicating urgency. Sandi hurried.

Doug met Sandi at the receptionists' desk and then took her to the conference room, where the supervisor gathered them in. A high school counselor had brought Maddie to the building by now, but because the realty office was inside a well-secured complex, Maddie was having trouble getting in. A maintenance worker on the inside finally saw her pacing in front of the main doors and let her in. While Maddie made her way to the realty office, Doug broke the news to Sandi.

"There has been a truck fire."

Sandi screamed, "Seth!"

The receptionist brought Maddie into the conference room. Doug made her take a seat. He was going to tell her something important. There had been a truck fire. Maddie screamed and vomited. (It would not be the only time she reacted that way.) She went out of her mind and screamed and screamed – for much longer than her brother might possibly have screamed during the remarkably brief time it took to succumb to smoke and the lethal gases it contained. Maddie screamed in pain for much, much longer than it took for my grandpa's fellow worker to be vanquished in an instant by the fire blowing out of the coal mine shaft. In fact, for a long, long time Maddie would battle the kind of pain Seth planned to escape.

Seth never figured this into his careful calculations, or he might have taken measures to make his departure more acceptable. But there was no harmless way to kill himself. No matter how he did it, he would force unthinkable suffering on his loved ones. That's why he couldn't think about them too much. Sticking a bowie knife through his neck was also unthinkable. He considered it many times, and he feared he would not be able to push it all the way in to finish the job. He didn't want to hang himself, either. The thought of dangling alive and not quite dead was unreasonable and terrifying. Poison wouldn't do for someone who loved good food and drink. Besides, it had failed for others and might fail for him. The last thing he needed was an indescribable migraine with indescribable nausea. Jumping from a high place did not appeal to him. He might not drown in the water if he hurled himself off a bridge, and he might only break his bones if he went off the top of a building. Shooting himself in the head was not a good choice either. There was nothing creative about it, nothing interesting to plan out. Same with sitting in the truck and letting carbon monoxide overtake him – unless it didn't. These were the thoughts he welcomed, not forlorn guesses about how his decision might affect other people. And yet, by insisting on a method that deserved careful, creative thought, Seth ended up thinking about the impact of each option. No matter how he did it, no matter how untidily or how neatly, the effects on others would be the same.

But maybe not for long, not very long, he said, he wondered, he hoped.

He had been considerate enough to park the truck where no other vehicles or property would be harmed. And he had parked by the fire hydrant. By the time he was ready to act on his plan, nothing could persuade him to rethink it. That is, nothing in himself. He was too far into a deep, dark zone to extract himself by his own strength. He was lunging beyond the point of no return, where desperate souls whimper and languish through days that won't go away, days that keep returning, one upon the other, in dreadful similarity and vacancy, in slow motion toward goals that race away from them, imparting full-blown confidence that good things will never be had.

Doug's brother and mother arrived at the realty office, received the news with horror, and then drove Doug, Sandi and Maddie to Doug's mother's house, some 15 miles away. There, Doug had more phone conversations with the detective and other police, while Sandi notified family and friends of the accident. It was an accidental truck fire. There was no other way to explain it. Also, the ignition switch was bad, or it was recently.

Ninety minutes later, the Murphys went home. People from their church brought food and plenty of it for several days. Most of them didn't know how to respond or talk to the Murphys in their shock and grief, but of course most of us have a natural craving to say and do something. Conversations were sometimes clumsy and a little irrelevant, but the Murphys found the efforts meaningful. The food provisions were a big help.

After a few days of faithful visitors in her house, Sandi was still numb but able to notice an aggregated effect of sad faces. She almost said, "Y'all look like somebody died!"

SETH'S LETTER

Seth became a little giddy as he pondered his plan to destroy his body. His relatively simple life had become, inside his head, unmanageably complex. Suicide was a seductive method of simplification. The note the detective found on his computer was a long one that told of a long 29 years of hard luck – failure in friendships, failure to find a girl to marry and love forever, failure in college, failure to deserve the promotion he was given at a Wal-Mart on the north side of Chicago. (He said the promotion fell in his lap as a stroke of luck.) He said his nearly unbroken history of bad luck might result in a failure even to take his own life.

Intertwined with a hundred dismal observations on his competence, most of which were repetititious misinterpretations of his experiences, was the promise of an end to what he called a miserable existence of hiding his fears and regrets and persistent depression behind a mask. He regretted the sorrow that his decision would bring to friends and family, but friends would forget him within a year, he said, and family, well, he had given that some thought, too:

I really am sorry for what I'm about to put you all through. I know you will never fully understand why I did what I did, but just understand I didn't come to this decision in haste, I didn't do it as a spur of the moment thing. I've considered everyone's reactions to my death, and I already feel terrible for what you're about to face, but at this point, I don't really care anymore. I'm not happy doing this, but I will save myself from a lifetime of depression this way.

In the end, the people it will affect most will be my family, of course. They'll cry. I'm not really proud of that fact, but it's going to happen regardless. ... I've managed to contribute nothing to this world. I've made no positive impact on anyone's life. ... I'll be a blurb in a newspaper, and then gone forever.

Seth clearly had not thought through the mess he would leave behind. He would not be a mere blurb in the news and then gone forever. He would live on in agitated memories of the people who would continue loving and missing him. His repeated self-denouncements were attempts to justify his decision to finally follow through with a plan. He scolded himself at length for failing to carry out many previous decisions to end his life.

He explained his plan for this Friday the 13th and his high hopes of acting upon it. He felt confident he would.

So, now on to the specifics. I have in my truck right now two gallons of gas. I plan on sitting in my truck, douse myself in gas, and set myself on fire. It's really going to hurt. A lot. I'm not looking forward to that portion, actually. You may wonder why I'm doing this in my truck. I need the extra fuel for the fire. If I were to just set myself on fire in the parking lot, there's a chance I'd just manage to damage and still somehow survive the process, whereas in my truck there will be plenty to keep the fire going until I am nothing more than ashes, in theory at least, not like I've done this before. Also keeping the fire relatively contained should not only keep collateral damage down, but decrease the time it takes for me to die. I'll suffocate to death before the fire kills me, and keeping myself contained will speed up the process.

Seth Murphy was sure that two gallons of gasoline poured on himself and the truck's interior would knock him out in a hurry, even though he said he "felt a bit of fear at the unknown." Earlier in his note he said he had chosen the "most painful method," but a few days later he was comfortable with the odds that he would be overtaken quickly by breathing poisonous smoke devoid of oxygen. Soon he would execute the strategy and then set the emptied gas can outside the truck. By the time the fire hoses swept it away, the man in the truck, with the seat leaned all the way back, would finally have succeeded at something he considered important and necessary – and which he admitted he didn't really want to do.

He also admitted that the reason his depression had progressed so far was that he thought he could conquer it on his own. It was another devastating miscalculation, because he didn't have any suitable thoughts to fight the depression. His own words were evidence:

I've lost the battle with my depression. Deep down, I always knew I would. … I've always wanted to go out in a blaze of glory.

His logic was fatally twisted: (1) He wanted to whip his depression on his own. (2) He could not. (3) So, whipping it was impossible.

In reality, Seth's need was for a new way of thinking. He complained of boredom and discussed the danger of his boredom. "All it allows me to do is think, and that leads to questions" about only negative things. Why should he try? Why should he care? Why didn't he get it all over with years ago? Why should he expect to enjoy the same pleasures of life that others do? He already had the negative answers, but the same old questioning kept coming back. "It's never good," he said. He was bored because he forced the same pessimistic analysis on everything in his life. The reason nothing good would happen was that nothing good would happen. He was self-stuck, and met his recurring bouts of depression with the same boring thoughts.

There could never be progress as long as he wanted to wage his battle alone and in what he called darkness. His entire problem was, in a very real way, simple and normal. It was simple in that the road to anyone's progress is a step at a time; he was fixated on ALL the problems he ever had. His problem was normal in that we all have similar challenges and disappointments and we all need support.

Seth's chosen solution, simple as it seemed to him, unleashed highly complex catastrophe on others, especially because the person at the center of their heartbreak had permanently made himself unavailable.

Somewhere along the line, Seth had contorted one of his parents' life principles according to his inward, negative thinking.

One of my beliefs that has been engrained into my core personality is the belief that everyone is more important than I am. That in the end, everyone else's happiness is more important than mine, and what other people want is more important than what I want. …

The core of that belief is a good one, one that everyone should have, but I seem to have taken it to an extreme. As a result, I can't stop thinking about the affect killing myself will have on the people around me. The pain my family will feel, the confusion and anger of my friends.

Seth wanted to ditch that concern long enough to end everything – end it all in a fiery flash and give everyone an early start on getting over him. On one hand, he could imagine that he would be missed, and on the other, he predicted he would be that fleeting blurb in the news. He couldn't stand being nagged by thoughts of other people's sadness over his death. He wished he hadn't been taught to care at all about them. His plan to destroy his depression would never succeed if he thought in detail about the effects of killing himself. And so he didn't. He was too far into the darkness to see very far around him. Besides, he had never done this before. Visibility was extremely poor. Seth Murphy just could not see more than a few feet in any direction. He was whacked out by depression.

THE ONE WITH THE PROBLEM

The head is a bad place to keep things that are bad for it. Seth was showing nervous ticks during middle school, and his parents thought a doctor should evaluate the condition. When Sandi took him to the appointment, the doctor said, "There's nothing wrong with him. He's a healthy boy."

Doug and Sandi weren't convinced. Their son had migraines in addition to the ticks. So Sandi took him to a specialist, who told her, "He's fine. You're the one with the problem."

That's part of the reason why Doug and Sandi still beat themselves up with guilt on a regular basis. Doug did his best as a father, but wonders if he did. Sandi replays everything in Seth's life. She says,

I was doing the best I could, but I don't think it was good enough.

When I read Seth's blogs, I get angry that nobody else was listening to me during his middle school years and nobody helped. I look back and see when my child was struggling. I tried to get him help, Doug tried. If Seth had told us he needed help, we would've done anything. He had an academic scholarship. His goal was to be a computer game designer.

And now, Sandi says, "I second-guess every decision I made with him."

She found some posts on social media that Seth had written almost 10 years earlier, during college. One of them tells why he basically hated his mother (the one who had tried to get him help for his mental distress long ago). Sandi knew Seth did not intend that she read the posts. Perhaps he forgot to remove the typical collegiate analysis of parents and their child-rearing performance. Seth was talkative on the web and posted hundreds of comments and blogs. Only a few are left, and each one is precious to his mother. She told me, "I think I like having it out there, because it's a piece of him. Even if the words are harsh toward me, it's the last piece I've got."

I know of a big, strong man who picked on a man half his size. The little man had a sophisticated social structure behind him, while the big man worked on his own power, unaware of the hidden mechanisms associated with the little man. One week later, the big man was found dead.

Seth was no match for a multidimensional force like depression. He knew help was available, he knew he needed it, and he hated his inability to beat depression on his own. It made him feel weak and incompetent, a hopeless loser. It was all in his head, all right, and that exactly was the problem. He was not "fine," as the specialist assured Sandi he was, and he had not been fine for years. Through one side of his mouth he said, "But I had given up years ago on coming close to being happy." Through the other side he said, "Tried again recently, failed, but it was nice to have hope again." He stumbled along on his own power, losing power along the way, until he arrived at his weakest point:

So I ask you, What would you do if you knew you only had one day left to live? Personally I woke up, watched some Stargate SG-1, went to work, for whatever reason, had a burger and some beer, and finished with more SG-1. It was a normal day for me.

It was a normal day for the man who once again stated that there was no chance for improvement. No matter what he might try, it would fail. No matter what "sliver of hope" was left, he was tired of slivers. They never panned out and they never would. So why hope? Why try, when everything was going to cave in anyway? Hope had left him, and the vacuum that replaced it sucked the life out of every dream he had.

It was all in his head, and hopeless thoughts make big men small. He tried to let everyone off the hook by saying they weren't to blame and couldn't have stopped his plan. That was no relief from the crushing burden of guilt his family would carry for as many years as Seth said he had suffered. He may as well have murdered his dad, who has borne a weight of sorrow and regret that he can never sit down and discuss with his son. Seth slammed the door shut on any chance of it.

DOUG'S PROBLEM

Seth hoped everyone would get over him as quickly as possible, but human memory is no pushover. Whenever Sandi has a problem with an electronic device, she remembers Seth's skills with cell phones, computers, and other devices, and she thinks, *I need to talk to Seth about this.* Then she remembers she can't. Every time she remembers him, she remembers she can no longer call him.

One of Doug's problems is the grill in the back yard. He and his son had great times cooking out there, bonding a little more each time – and they were already close. Now the grill reminds Doug that Seth lit himself like a stack of charcoals gone wild. Now the grill reminds Doug that Seth is gone. Now the grill reminds Doug that maybe he did a thousand things wrong and should've been a much better dad. That's how most dads are. But Doug can't do a thing about it, and sometimes Sandi hears him in the garage turning the air blue with vocabulary that doesn't mean anything but "Why did you have to do that, Seth? You didn't have to do that! I miss you so badly, son! What did I do wrong? What could I have done differently to make you feel loved enough and important enough to stick around instead of trying to turn yourself into a heap of ashes? This is killing me. You killed *me*, Seth! We're in this together!"

Christmas Eve became difficult. The Murphys' tradition was as follows: Doug read the Nativity story from the Bible and *'Twas the Night Before Xmas*, and Seth read *The Polar Express*. Then the Murphys would exchange one gift and go to bed. Sandi explained the new effort:

> On the first Christmas after Seth's death, we had a big debate about whether we'd read *The Polar Express*. I said I wanted to do it. I tried it but couldn't. Doug's mom finished, but it was horrible, not the same. We decided not to read it the next Christmas.

Seth's evaluation of his effect on everyone else's life didn't even scratch the surface of the deep reserves of human memory. No matter how he might have chosen to end his life, the desolation and hurt he left his loved ones would be unforgettable and beyond measure.

Doug described the mess in response to three questions I said I knew would be asking him to twist a dagger in his heart: (1) How did he feel the day he adopted Sandi's son? (2) Why was the love between him and Seth so obvious to everyone? (3) What kind of mess had Seth left him?

> The day Seth died was the hardest, most horrible day of my life. When I found out, first there was denial, then a hurting and sadness that I don't even know words to begin to describe it. Then I had to travel for about an hour to tell Sandi and Maddie. I was mostly numb for the rest of that day and many after. Without family and friends who trust in God, I'm not sure we could have gotten through those first days after Seth died.
>
> We didn't find out Seth had committed suicide until a month later. I took the detective's call. After I hung up, I think I went into shock. I was numb and shaking. If Seth's death still seemed unreal, how could the latest news possibly be true?

Sometimes I still don't completely believe it. A mental mess is one way to describe it. Confusion, sadness, anger, unbelieving, self-torture (what had I done wrong? where did I fail Seth as a father?) all mixed up into the darkest, blackest soup you could imagine.

I have so many emotions about this. They vary from day to day, but they are always there. And they are all bad. I guess the most overwhelming emotion I feel is a sadness so deep I can hardly bear it. Just the realization that my son, my Seth, was in such pain and I never knew it. I don't know what I should have done. I just know I should have done something. I will never stop blaming myself for this. The not knowing. Whether this is rational or not, I do not know. It just is.

I will live with this the rest of my life. But there are other emotions or messes as well. Probably the worst is what I call the darkness. It may be what others would call depression. It is like being at the bottom of a deep, dark well and there is no light, just stifling, stale air and I am surrounded by it. Actually, all of the emotions are probably the worst. There are times I will be in a room and panic will set in. It is all I can do not to just bolt from the room and take off. To where I do not know, but just to get away from where I am.

And Yes I Do Feel Anger. Why didn't Seth let us know something was wrong? We would have done anything in the world to help him. There is the mess it has made of all of our lives, Sandi's, Maddie's, and mine. We will never heal the scars this has left on our hearts.

I still talk to Seth. I tell him I love him and miss him. I ask him why. I have been screaming in the shower for two years. I'm not sure it helps, but I still do it.

WHAT SANDI SAW

Two years after Seth's passing, his mother took the day off work to brace for the second anniversary of the burning of the 1998 Mazda pickup. At work the next day, feeling melancholy, she popped a CD into a player and listened to an ABBA song she liked, *Cassandra*. Two co-workers whose offices were near hers came into Sandi's office to listen. She asked if they knew of the Greek mythological character, Cassandra. Neither of them did.

When Sandi returned home, she decided to refresh her own memory of Cassandra. She turned on the computer and looked her up online. As she read about her, she remembered a one-act play she had cut when she was the debate coach at a local high school. The play was "The Curse of Cassandra." Sandi explains:

> It was an obscure play, and we had a copy of it at the old high school where I had helped, where Seth attended. He was on the debate team, and he and another student performed the funny cutting. Cutting is the process of reducing a piece to its core in order to fit the time constraints of a competition. This involves literally taking scissors and cutting out the parts you don't need for the presentation.

Sandi began missing her son as she refreshed her memories about Cassandra.

I had liked the one act. As I was searching for information on Cassandra, I found a copy of the one-act play and, to my surprise, I found a comment posted on it. I looked at the name of the person who knew the play, and saw "Sethmurp", which is a pseudonym Seth often used. The name was hyperlinked. I clicked on it and was taken to a blog site.

The first entry I saw was the last one he had written on that site. My heart skipped a beat when I read it.

> (Dated Sept 22, 2006) Yes,Yes, I still exist. And I bring chemical goodness.

I had discovered a blog he had written over a two-year time period, which included his time at the university before he flunked out.

After talking with Sandi, I performed a search myself and found that Seth had updated his user profile on another website. His redundant self-denunciations included the following:

> Once upon a time I was a typical university guy but dozed all the way through. No problem, because now I'm flipping yummy burgers and working part time in the Wal-Mart electronics department.

He added:

> :'(

That bare-boned graphic represented what he would say five and a half years later in his farewell address – that he was a disgusting loser in college. He told his kid sister in one of their last conversations, "Don't be like me. Go to college and graduate." But he was not interested in sticking around to cheer her on. He was going to leave her the worst example a big brother could leave, and he, the gentle warrior who earned a first-degree black belt in karate by the end of 8th grade, didn't want to think about the effects his plan would have on her or anybody. "It had been a long time coming," he said, and after many disappointing attempts to muster the courage to go through with it, because he had let himself be affected by thoughts of the sadness he would cause for others, he was sure he was going to be able to forget all about them and make it happen this time, with as much irony as he could pack into it. The plan was in place, the courage was in place, and he felt a calm about his determination. He contemplated his options for the finishing touches, savoring them with a measure of understandable excitement. Hardly anything else made him feel good anymore, and nothing made him feel good for long.

I woke up this morning with the intent to end my life. I had planned on doing it earlier, after I got off work, but I decided to wait until after midnight. I've always had a thing for the number 13, seems like a nice little touch there, if I say so myself.

CLEANING OUT SETH'S APARTMENT

The Murphys and two friends went to Seth's apartment in Chicago the day after his memorial service to gather his possessions and bring them back to the Murphys' garage in Stickney. Doug found a bubble-padded package addressed to Seth. He squeezed it and opened it.

"He got this for me!" Doug yelled, holding a T-shirt in the air. It combined two of Doug's favorite things – the Beatles and The Lord of the Rings. Seth knew his dad would love it. The front showed profiles of the four Lord of the Ring Hobbits in a Beatles-like foursome. The caption underneath said: The Fab Four.

The T-shirt hadn't arrived in time for Seth to give it to Doug for his birthday on January 5th, which was another serious miscalculation in more than one way. Not only did his dad receive the gift on a day that Seth had forced into infamy, but the gift would remain a reminder of loss even after someday becoming, as we must hope that it will, an undisputed reminder of how much Seth loved his dad.

In his departure note, Seth wrote that he didn't want to kill himself on New Year's Eve, because

I didn't want to spoil the holiday and my dad's birthday, both of which would have been marred forever.

He was able in that moment to see the distance that pain could travel into the future, and yet he could not see that his plan would compel his family to grieve every New Year's Eve in his absence. His very note would make sure of that, once they had read it. And they would grieve his absence every January 5th. Eight days later they would have the pleasure of grieving the 13th. Three additional, appalling miscalculations!

The Murphys don't have space in their house for all the belongings they brought back from their son's apartment. Some of his things never left the Murphy's attic in the first place. Most of his clothes have been given away. Friends were invited to take whatever they wanted. We'll see how they feel about it after they learn the truth. Sandi doesn't want to look at the stuff. She says to sell it all, get rid of it, get it out of sight, whatever it takes. Doug and Maddie want to go through it first, when they can get in the mood. All that stuff is a piece of Seth, and the process is part of the debris the guy with the heart of a kitten bequeathed to them.

THE COUNSELING EXPERIENCE

The week after Seth's death, the Murphys began four weeks of counseling with a licensed professional. That counselor played an indispensable role in Maddie's recovery, which Doug and Sandi made their top priority. They had been caught off guard by their son's condition; they would not allow that to happen with their daughter.

Two very important things were accomplished with Maddie. First, the counselor recommended that she become involved in art therapy under the guidance of a certain agency. Maddie soon discovered that she liked art and that she could use it as an effective coping tool when she felt bad. Sandi calls the counselor's suggestion "immensely helpful."

Second, the counselor advised Doug and Sandi on how to break the news of the suicide to their daughter. The solution reflected an intelligent understanding of how memory can be protected from unintended, repulsive associations. Doug and Sandi took Maddie to a neutral place, a place with which she had no prior experience. There they told her the truth. She vomited. After they took her home, she vomited again. But the wisdom of the solution is that none of her familiar or cherished places were ruined by being connected to the news that rocked the foundations of her life.

Maddie continued art therapy and began seeing a psychiatrist specialized in her condition and who was able to prescribe a controlled amount of medication that has continued to be reduced over time. Maddie is not ashamed for you to know this.

The financial reality of mental health is that proper treatment can be expensive and insurance coverage is often much less than the bill. Doug and Sandi had to make a decision. They were willing to go into debt, if necessary, to get Maddie whatever help was necessary. They would have done the same for Seth if they had known of his need. Medication is another formidable expense. And there were three Murphys in need of a recovery program. Sandi puts their dilemma in honest terms:

> As the medications helped Maddie cope, she has been able to cut down on the frequency of her visits, and we have a little more money for Doug and me to put toward our own visits to the psychiatrist.

> I do not have an answer to the issue of affordability. We are struggling to pay the difference between what insurance pays and what the doctor charges.

> As for ourselves, I guess Doug and I are just holding on as best we can. I don't know how long I will see the psychiatrist. It depends on funds. I just hope the two of us can get to a point where we are functioning better than we have been.

The Murphys are doing what they can. As with other major health conditions, difficult choices must be made. Putting off proper attention can lead to long-term struggles that don't resolve themselves. Recovery may involve going into debt in order to live life well. Or treatments may be staggered according to the ability to pay. Patients may also be able to negotiate a sliding-scale payment plan or obtain financial assistance. In any case, the value of a restored life is far above the cost of restoration. Just ask the Murphys. They would gladly give anything to bring their son back.

The Murphys continue working toward restoration. If they had the money, they all would have placed themselves under the thorough care of a professional by now. They are doing what they feel is most reasonable in managing their overall stress load. But they do not believe that money is the answer. Says Sandi:

> Some wealthy families have given their sons the best mental health help they could afford, yet their sons still committed suicide.

Seth put his parents in a tough spot. They are weary. They are always weary. And weariness casts a draining gloom on life. Sandi hopes her son is resting in peace, but she's not enjoying the same benefit. Seth's actions resulted in her developing sleep apnea and now she sleeps with the assistance of a machine, while Doug is struggling immensely every day to find a reason to get up and get going.

MADDIE'S MESS

Maddie still has dreams once a week or so in which Seth shows up, as if he never died, as if the family only thought he did, and now he's back. Sometimes the dreams are so real to Maddie that she *knows* he's back. Other times, she realizes she's dreaming and she tries to talk to him – in a conscious dream, you might say. But she never remembers much when she fully awakens.

He's still in my life every day. I went through a deep depression after he passed. My parents don't know how bad some of those nights were. I was close to making the same mistake Seth made. Asking for help was one of the hardest things I have ever done, but there aren't any words that can tell how grateful I am for the help I got.

Even after fighting the depression and coming out on top, I still wake up from those dreams frequently. I also see things that remind me of him everyday, and my heart breaks when I realize how he will never threaten to beat up my boyfriend, cry at my graduation, or spoil my future kids to pieces.

I always looked up to him. I had to; I'm pretty short. He was always so big and strong. Nothing could knock him down. I never questioned the fact he would always be here with me, but I didn't know it was a question in his mind.

After I found out how he died, I didn't understand how he could just leave. How he could just be gone and never come back. How he could make that kind of decision and leave me. I thought he loved me.

Was I that bad of a sister? Of course after his passing I blamed myself, like everyone does. I didn't know why he didn't get help, because it sounded so simple in my mind at that time. I now know its a lot harder than it sounds, but still, he should have gotten help. He should have talked to me, his roommate, my mom, a random volunteer on the suicide line, anyone.

Seth bestowed a terrible mess upon his sister. His depression did not end after all. He gave it to Maddie. He handed it off like a baton for her to run with for as long as she would need to run before she could unload it with help from professionals, family, and friends, something he chose not to do. Maddie continues:

Depression has taken its toll on my self-image. I'm more self-conscious, kind of paranoid, or maybe nervous about myself. I mean, if my own brother thought I was that horrible to leave me, I must have been.

Relationships have been hard too. I'm always scared of my long-term boyfriend leaving me just like Seth did. It's little things too. People joke about "it" all of the time and don't think twice. A math test coming up? "Kill me now," I hear from across the classroom. I can never bring my self to say the "S-word". Even though I'm not thinking about him all of the time like I used to, he's always there – in the back of my mind. Sometimes he's my funny big brother. Other times he's the guy who left me and isn't coming back.

When Maddie first started art therapy, she had no idea she could learn to draw.

When the program started I hadn't told anyone how Seth really died; it was my biggest secret. The instructor told us of a

Maddie Murphy was 15 when she drew this award-winning picture of a happy memory of Seth. Title: Bubby. Media: pen and ink and wash.

technique she often used. You create a random code and then write it on paper or canvas, and then you paint and tape and you glue pictures over it.

I tried it. It became the first time I had told the truth about my brother. I was just telling a piece of paper. I covered *that word* up with so many layers of paint and tape and pictures. No one but me knew it was there. Now I have many friends who know and support me when I need it, but at the time it was such a weight lifted off my shoulders when I wrote *that word* down.

Maddie transferred to another high school the next year and studied under "an amazing art teacher."

She helped me realize I wasn't too bad when I had some guidance with freedom to do what I wanted. I was assigned the project I did of me and Seth a few weeks before his birthday, and was working on it the day before his first birthday without him here. I had made a new friend in the class who didn't know anything about my brother.

A boy sitting across from Maddie at the art table was pointing out her mistakes as she worked on her Bubby drawing. His behavior, which is not unusual for high school boys, produced an unforeseen result that Maddie now values.

I started crying. The girl I was becoming friends with had no idea why. I blurted out between the sobbing, "He's dead!"

I then went to the bathroom and called my dad to come get me. I always stress out before I finish a piece. This was the worst one, but it helped to cry, just to get it out. I had been holding the feelings in the whole time I was doing the drawing. I wasn't crying or feeling anything. I was numb. In that moment though, it all came out. Every heartbreaking moment of the past eight months came out.

Maddie fought much of her depression the way many people do – alone. In the process, she resorted to inflicting injury on herself through a method called cutting.

This is the hardest topic for me to talk about – me cutting myself. When I think of how far I've come since then, I can't believe I cut myself. But it's a part of my past, and makes me who I am today. My parents had no idea what was going on. I made it sort of obvious at times when I rolled up my sleeves, but they never noticed or maybe they only saw what they wanted to see.

I remember one night that was horrible. I was sobbing on the guest bed in the back bedroom and cutting with anything I could find. I wanted to run across the street to the neighborhood pond and just end it then and there. I knew I couldn't, though, and I knew I needed to talk to a close friend of mine. I texted what seemed like a book and told her everything. She told me she had felt the same way a year ago when her family was having problems. She told me it would get better, and even if I didn't believe her at the time, her words made me make it through that meltdown.

Why I was cutting I don't know. I just had this urge to do it. I felt numb. I knew it was bad and that I shouldn't, but I did anyway. I told myself that I would just stop later, but things escalated. Like I said before, asking for help was the hardest thing I have ever done. When I told my parents, at first I just told my mom it was with a bobby pin, so she doesn't know how bad I really was and how close some of those nights were to losing another child.

Sometimes I still have the urge to cut, and I'll admit I slipped up once since, but I now know I am stronger than this illness. I don't think this depression will ever fully go away. When my parents don't agree with decisions I make, when I get a really bad grade, or when I get into a bad fight with a close friend it comes back, but I'm able to calm down better now. I cry a lot, I'll say that straight up, but that's healthy. That's how I let out the feelings. And I also am completely honest with those closest to me so I don't have to carry burdens by myself.

I am so grateful for telling someone, now that I have gotten through this. I now have an amazing boyfriend, good grades, honors clubs, and great friends. It wasn't easy, but I now know how strong I really am.

This is Maddie's mess. She's working through something she never would have had to work through if Seth had been able to see far enough ahead and measure his impact on the family's future.

WHAT THE POLICE STILL DON'T KNOW

Shortly after 12 a.m. on Friday the 13th, Sandi opened the passenger door of the 1998 Mazda pickup and climbed into the tight space. Seth's seat was as far from the steering wheel as he could get it. He was tilted a bit because the seatback was slightly out of joint. It was always out of joint. Seth didn't care; he liked that truck. He had the same problem it had.

The windows were down. Sandi figured it was for feeding oxygen to the fire. The gas can was on the floorboard leaned against his right knee. He had moved it so she could get in. It had enough fuel in it to reduce himself to ashes, which he said we're all destined to be eventually. Sandi sat terrified, speechless, far too late to do anything about something that happened a month ago, two months ago, six months ago, 18 months ago, two years ago, next year and the year after that.

She could only watch and scream soundlessly – or sometimes out loud when she was in her car or home alone. She begged him not to do it, not to pour it, not to light it. This was the woman who carried him for more than nine months and then took a week to deliver. The doctors congratulated her on giving birth to a toddler. He was big even then, and Sandi had never experienced such joy as when he was first placed in her arms.

The nurses propped him up in a pumpkin seat so he could watch them, because he wouldn't sleep like the other newborns. He was already preparing to chart his own course with endless curiosity about the world around him, in the United States and Europe. He became a voracious reader and had the heart of a kitten. Anyone who knew him became his friend. He enjoyed being with his sister and would listen intently to her latest, rambling epic of life in high school.

As Sandi always did, she begged Seth not to start the fire. He was behaving as though he were still in his pumpkin seat. What she ought to do is call 911 and have the emergency crew stop this nonsense. But it had already happened. She knew she was wasting her breath. So once again she had to get out of the truck and let her son have his way. A mother cannot watch those kinds of things. It was always so sad to walk away again and not be able to talk him out of it. Today, tomorrow, next year she will climb back into the truck and try again. Seth's dad will too.

Sometimes Sandi screams in her car on the way home from work, on the way back to Stickney, where only a few people know what really happened. Some police friends know.

The truth about the truck will come out with this book, but Doug, Sandi and Maddie believe that their story, having been told in a truthful and straightforward manner, will be more important than their secrecy.

Meanwhile, Sandi shrieks in the car.

ABOUT THE AUTHOR

Max T. Russell was named after a great-grandfather who hanged himself in a barn. A grandson of that man later shot himself dead. A week later, the grandson's father succumbed to extreme grief. Then that man's wife, the author's great aunt, lived another 30-some years without a father, a husband, and a son.

Max T, his identical twin, Max S, and Luke W Russell, create a variety of information products for homes, businesses and schools. Here are a few of their websites:

ReachingTheLatinos.com - How businesses, organizations and politicians can reach Latino immigrants.

maxtrussell.com - Marketing IT and BI in-house.

THE SETH MURPHY SCHOLARSHIP

Upon Seth's death, the Murphys established a scholarship fund in his name at the high school where he graduated – the same one Maddie attends.

The Murphys asked sympathizers to donate to the fund instead of buying flowers for his funeral. They received enough to get the scholarship going for a few years, awarding $500 each spring to a senior wanting to pursue a career in a computer-related or technology-related field.

Do you want to help keep Seth's scholarship fund operating in the future? It encourages students who share his interests to move forward and do what he always wished he had done.

To find out how to make a direct donation to the fund, write me at:
maxt@maxtrussell.com

National Suicide Prevention Hotline

1-800-273-8255

http://www.suicidepreventionlifeline.org

Depression, Fear, Loneliness, Shame and Disappointment can drive people to consider ending their lives. Trained counselors should be sought out to properly deal with these emotions.

Never be ashamed to ask for help. Don't try to bulldoze your way through by yourself. We all need help getting through tough times.